T0196527

FORTY-EIGHT

FORTY-EIGHT

Ann Ibarra

FORTY-EIGHT

iUniverse books may be ordered through booksellers or by contacting:

iUniverse
1663 Liberty Drive
Bloomington, IN 47403
www.iuniverse.com
1-800-Authors (1-800-288-4677)

ISBN: 978-1-5320-5499-0 (sc)
ISBN: 978-1-5320-5498-3 (e)

Library of Congress Control Number: 2018910952

Print information available on the last page.

iUniverse rev. date: 09/14/2018

I am strength
loved
myself
guided
beautiful
I am enough

Revived

Sun Burning bright
Drowning in warmth
Leaving its mark
Over my North
Body half naked
Red rubber bands
Covering parts
In water and sand
White fluffy tide
Coming up close
Gliding like birds
On this salty coast
Watery pellets
Poking my eyes
Flying up high
White butterflies
Jumping and leaping
Ballet performs
Leaping and jumping
Thighs feeling warm
Laughing and screaming and losing control,
Tossing and turning my watery soul
Coming for air I laugh on the sand,
Spring has arrived
I live once again.

Coincidence?

A Chance meeting with, your new fallen ex
Who lives, breathes, and walks, -- won't cease to exist...
You knew what you'd see, if you saw my eyes
The truth in my gaze, remembering lies
You knew that I'd see, the love we once had
Still there in your heart, that now had gone bad.
But why then, do you, take chances like these
To visit my friends where you knew I'd be?
They hate what you've done, to their frail friend
Who isn't quite well, and still on the mend
Did you come to brag? Are you full of hate?
That you'd punish me, in my weakest state?
Or....
Was this a ploy to see me again?
To get that last chance to hold my sweet hand?

Message From a Groom

We parted because the distance was hard
It felt like a burden that pulled us apart
We parted as many--Young lovers do
I searched for new love in all that I knew
No matter the woman, the face, or the place
I never would find, the one to replace
My one, true, sweet love that filled my life's graces
With overabundance of loving embraces.
I looked for her there, I looked for her here
I looked for her where, she did not appear.
I yearned for that feeling of joy that she gave
And packed up my pride then traveled that day
To see my true love, and ask her forgiveness
To make her my bride, and make all my witness
To true love that grows, that fades, but not dies
That weakens and suffers, then blows in the cries
Of cold that must kill, disease in the air
Of fighting and hurting and cheating unfair
But love comes again, as all seasons do
With brightness of sun for flowers that bloom
This love that once laid in dormant surrender
Did creep out of death and frigid, cold winter
But sunshine and warmth, from true lover's hand
Was all that was needed for spring to expand.

Stracylove

We met in the garden of towering trees
In northern cool summers of Californ' breeze
She crept from the loft
Where she often slept
And gave me a look
Most certainly dread
Her fear of me lingered
But just for a second.
I went up to hold her
In love as I beckoned.
I asked,
"What's her name?"
You said, "Tracylove"
And you watched as she carefully came from above.
Her story was awful,
Sweet and amazing
I listened in awe
Of this kitty's taking
Of one of her lives
As cats have but nine
It wasn't without true love that was kind.
He saw but a flash
Her black fur and white
---leap from the woods
With dinner in sight
For she was a stray
A young wild cat

Who hunted for food
In woods where she napped
But tires and steel
Would scare her that day
And crush her poor hips
And hurt her that way.
An angel did lift her
From death's dark embrace
She saw how he saved her
And remembered his face
The doctor was hopeless
And wrote her away
But He wouldn't have it
He wouldn't that day
See, his father had passed
Just one year before
And the suffering lingered
In his heart's sad door
So into his life
His Tracy did come
She lived for the man
Who saved her heart's drum.
For weeks did he visit
To clean out her body
And stroke her soft fur
That was short and still stubbly
The doctors were struck
by this little life
That wouldn't stop living
For she was his wife
She loved this sweet man
And gave it her all

A stray nevermore
For she was a ball
Of sweet loving fur
Of "meeps" and of paws
That lay on his legs
With sweet little claws
My baby is now
Asleep on her bed
She's spoiled and loved
And domestic instead
But let the moon rise
And let her heart race
She'll leap like a wave
To touch the sky's face!

The Ruse

"Where are our friends?" I asked you again.
You checked on your phone as if you had then,
A message from someone although you had none
No, they were not given, a notice to come...
So there we were two, on a rooftop alone
Together at once, in a romantic zone
How had this occurred? I wondered just then
But went quite along, I had to pretend
That I was ok with this date you devised
To have me alone, on this roof as a prize
We chatted a lot about reggae and jazz
You smoked just a few and spoke with pizazz
But all this whole time, I questioned your motives
On why we were there, on this rooftop with votives
Candles that sparkled and comfortable chairs
Tables that stacked up for reception flair!
You brought me my drinks, a vodka and sprite
And opened your eyes, when I stretched up that night
You saw just a glimpse, of my midriff just then
Your eyes gave a sparkle, I noticed your grin
The evening concluded--had been quite ambitious.
For the rooftop, the candles, were very suspicious
That this was a date, our first in the making
Never asked for in theory, just me for the taking...
Midnight had come and I was set to go
And you grabbed me at once, and you kissed me just so...
You tasted my face, you're tongue danced around

And I felt just a bit like escaping somehow
For, was this a date? Was I not deceived?
Was this all a ploy to get me indeed?
You kissed me again, as I looked at a star
And you licked my cheek once, then I sat in my car.
Were we not friends?! I was truly deceived!
So why did I watch you, as you turned to leave?
Now, *I* was curious, perplexed with dismay
Who was this man? Who kissed me this way?

Excess

You wouldn't come near me but spoke to all others
And asked all about me, asked what were my druthers
A train wreck just waiting, I wouldn't pretend
I felt little pity for drunken young men
You quietly left, out the door with your pride
To walk to your home and sleep there inside
Your legs helped you walk and then led you away
To stumble and fall on the sidewalk that day
You called me not once, not twice, but then thrice
And again and again and became quite a vice
That brought me discomfort and so close to fear
I handed the phone to a friend who was near
He told you "Be calm" And you asked him to say,
"Please tell her to call me" But I wouldn't that way.
I felt a great sadness for such a sweet man
Who couldn't quite function at spirit's dark hand
I liked that you liked me but knew in the end
That this was a problem that couldn't begin
The next day you wrote, a text so inclined to
send your apology and sorrow divine
I forgave your dark side but had to agree
That drunken behavior was awful to see
You swore off the liquor and stuck to less beer
A sacrifice now, that you cling to I hear…
I think we have vices, each one of us do
And long to be better,
I hope that is true.

Waiting

I wait for the spring to feel you again
To hold you and kiss you and mend every end
You don't know you're coming to see me this way
It's destined to happen; I'll wait for the day.
I'll see you sometime; I'll see you once more.
We'll see how in time our love is reborn
Our friendship will blossom when feelings abide
The love that we have, way hidden inside
And if I must wait for the next life to come
I will look for your hands and your voice, and your sun,
So find me my sweet; LOVE, find me once more!
Deep there in your heart, the one I adore.

Austin

I thought for a moment then gathered my things
And got in my car and flew as with wings
The drive was a long one, my buns were quite sweaty
The summer was sizzling and heat was quite steady.
You stood in the doorway, a cool glass of water
I tried to seem friendly without any bother.
You led me inside and said you would show
Some rapids not far from where we would go.
So off to the hills of Austin we went,
To cool off our bodies in water to drench
We hiked for a while, I laughed at your jokes
You took off your shirt; my eyes looked like "O"s.
This was to be friendly, a visit for friends
I wasn't quite sure, if I could depend
On myself that Monday, when heat was so warming,
And wine had been pouring through veins that were soaring
We drove up a hill that rocked your gold Jeep
I sprang to the window and started to sing
Your hand took my leg to keep me from falling
And feelings of comfort kept senses from calling
My prudish belief that good girls don't do this
Still, this fuzzy head was heading for bliss.
We found just the place, to set our things there
And swam into water that baptized our hair
This place felt like heaven; the water was rushing
Around our whole bodies my heart began crushing
Your eyes looked through mine; your lips came to me

I couldn't say no, your body agreed
I kissed your smooth lips; I felt your strong tongue
I wrapped legs around you and felt my heart strum.
You held me so closely; I felt your smooth skin
And placed my wet hands upon your sweet chin
Your golden hair glistened, your blue eyes, they sang
And water was rushing, my heart, how it rang!
Like bells in the belfry, on days to declare
The freedom of love and of life and of care!
You swam with me quickly to streams running fast
Where we could have time, to make moments last
I sat on your lap, as water surrounded
Our bodies with rapids, and passion abounded
I settled my life, in your hands that moment
And found all the love, that once left me dormant
You rescued me darling; I rescued you too
Then swam to our bed
And knew what to do

The Picture

I saw you in a picture
Your eyes were closed and puffy
Your hair was thin and dirty
Your beard was long and scruffy
I saw another picture
From when you were with me
A Christmas celebration
Around a Christmas tree.
You looked so smooth and healthy,
You looked so calm, serene
I loved you in that photograph
The one where you loved me
But now you're off with her
She has you that I see
You're not the same sweet man
So different now, to me
You used to bring me joy
I see that you have changed
My once strong, solid boy
You're distant, now estranged
I hope you're happy now,
The boy who once loved me
The golden, smiling boy
Under that Christmas tree

Movie Preview

"A movie…" you said, with a hesitant, "Yes,"
I found it more pleasing, than talking I guess.
In movies you sit and you watch and you stare
And nothing can cause any nervousness there.
So we went to the movies to say nothing more
So you would not find me, the least of a bore.
Mad Max was the movie, it had a great look
So into the theatre, we sat in a nook.
Not many were there in the mid-day we saw
And we sat in the darkness as I sipped with my straw.
The cars on the screen were cruising and grinding
My heartbeat was pulsing as your hand began winding
Your fingers, on my lap, as I looked ahead
I tried not to react, or turn my stunned head.
You never once moved, your hand from my leg
But fingers were creeping, I wanted to beg
For you to please stop, this circling motion
Your fingers were moving, like dizzying potion
Two hours of guessing, what moved through my mind?
You never once asked me, if I was the kind
To sit in a theater, dark as the night
And hold someone near, so closely and tight
Your fingers still moved one hour had passed
And gently they traveled, the motion did last

I uncrossed my legs to loosen your grip
You casually moved your fingers a bit.
Much higher than they had circled before
--Making their way, so close to my door.

Chimichangas

I ordered my soup
He ordered his platter; a full plate of
beans, burritos, and batter.
We ate and we talked like friends for some time
Then he blurted out words as I sucked on my lime.
"So what do you want?" He asked me like that.
I had not an answer, for this, so I sat.
I pondered a moment at what I should say
"Excuse me?" I answered and looked in dismay.
He wasn't my type. I knew this that moment.
Too calm and too quiet, too cute, and would torment
My thoughts every night that he'd be away
I had my suspicions, I had them that day.
They say calmer waters run deep and run wild
His manner was smooth and seemingly mild.
My hesitant manner was making him wait
He wasn't accustomed to unfulfilled dates.
He said he could feel it, this thing that we had
Just something between us! And then he looked sad.
I couldn't believe how this meal had come
From a moment of laughter to a friendship undone
I wouldn't be swayed by his sad confrontation
--too mature were my thoughts for his young generation.
The one where you think you deserve what you want
And you ask and you ask, 'Til you get what you haunt.
I still wasn't moved by his sad pouty mood.
Then he said something odd as I played with my food.

"Excuse me a moment---I need to go pee. (I
have a large penis---you may want to see.)
He left me alone, to ponder this thought.
I pondered and pondered and pondered a lot.
He came back in moments from being relieved and said
"We should go" then we got up to leave.
I smelled like a taco, he smelled like cologne
He held me so tightly then left me alone.
He played his game wisely and left me to see
If I was mistaken to let him go free

Alligator Tears

You asked me questions, accused me of,
A night when I was-- not in love
It wasn't you, I knew that much
For we were not the ones in touch
I knew you were, a friend of friends
But never knew intentions then.
I simply swam in darkened pool
It was one night and no one knew
I only kissed him but a while
And we were done, that's just my style.
Accusing someone who holds you now?
Who told him "Bye" One night was all
You cried a tear I was alarmed.
A man that cries had I just harmed?
Your tears did stream down from your face
My heart did break, I had to race
Upon your lap to kiss you there, to
kiss your skin that was so fair.
Your tears did fall upon my hand
I kissed you, held you, held your hand
You looked in shock that I should be
The one to hold you, yes, indeed!
I wounded you, not knowing how,
But thinking back, I can see now
That lovers never want to know

That once upon, a time ago
There was a past, when they were not
The one you had in hands and thoughts
Of love and laughter, quite insane

We never mentioned that again.

Pool Party

You kissed my lips to let all know
Then I was asked, "Is he your beau?"
I widely smiled, and had to say, "I guess
he is! I guess since May."
It was not something I could say
Just months ago or years away
I have a boyfriend! -- was my thought
He seems to love me, and a lot!
His pride did shine when I was there
With him that day and everywhere
I'd always been a girl you see
Just always lonely, sadly free
I longed to be on a young man's arm
And visit friends with girlfriend charm
We kissed that day in front of all,
Right in the pool in sunlight's thrall
He showed me off as if to say,
"She's mine all men! So stay away!"
I loved him more as he held me
I wish that all could let us be
In cool pool water on that day
I felt so proud and loved at bay.
Our friend did yell,"Hey! Get a room!"
And so we kept our actions prude.

I loved you so, I couldn't say
Until tonight when you're away
You were my love, my soulmate too.
Those were the days of skies so blue.

Wedding Stuff

This groom had had some trouble with
Relationships and bridal bliss
It was another story where
This couple split to her despair.
But after years of being apart
He found that she still had his heart
I met him once with other friends
This concert made all scream and bend
He seemed a shell, an empty soul
Who longed for her; she was his gold
And now he stood a happy man
With all around to witness then
The love that brought this wedding day
To never, ever go away

And as we watched and witnessed all
The Wedding and the lover's ball
My boyfriend turned and said to me
"Should we be married in Capri?"
My eyes grew wide, my hands grew sweaty
My heart went light, but were we ready?
What did I care? I told him "Yes…!"

I wonder, does he
Remember this…?

The Shower

So I was in the shower, so clean and in my power
You walked in without clothes; I was at once exposed!
You took a sponge and then, took soap into your hand
Together they made suds, and frothy bubble buds
You started down below, and washed my calves and toes
I tried to stay upright, and held your shoulder tight
Your hands moved up my leg, and made me take a breath
I saw your face so sweet, and then I washed your feet
I moved up to your thighs and looked up at your eyes
You washed my hair with hands that
moved my world like sands
That move from earthquakes shift, which crash just like a gift
As Earth's red molten core, bursts hot volcanoes' door
Your hands washed every part and stole my very heart
Such love, such care, you gave, my life you came to save!
We moved then to the bed, to kiss and hug instead
Still wet, still soapy too, you moved above me new
I took my fingers fair, to fe-el your wet hair
I brought you to my face and then began to taste
The love that you did feel, could this be truly real?
Was I already here? In love with you my dear?
Perhaps it was just sex and life is just a mix
Of moments where we tread, from shower into bed
So then I closed my eyes and tried to keep from lies
That said this could be real, then thought, "It's no big deal"
But then you whispered softly and sweetly in my ear
Those words that came at once, and told me not to fear

"I love you," you did say!
And turned my night to day
I said it back to you, I said
"I love you," too!
The passion wasn't done, as bodies became one
In flames that did combust from love and joy and lust.
We swirled for hours this way; I knew it from that day
That love can come this fast,
And yes, sometimes does last.

What Now?

You said you loved me, so did I
How could I walk away and sigh
To wonder if I was just one
Of many that you'd loved and done?
Were you just one of men who chose
To love them, lose them, and dispose?
Now what was I? A weekend fling?
A girl to be without a ring?
I'd been that girl in times before
And wanted just a little more.
I wanted that security,
Of being someone's love to see
If maybe somewhere down the line
We'd be like one for a long time.
And as we sat at Moonshines' bar
You told the man who stood not far
To make your "girlfriend" vodka sprite,
"That's what she'd like here for the night"
Girlfriend? ---Did I just hear him right?
Was I his girlfriend? Was I that night?
Was I no longer on my own?
Was his heart my brand new home?
Could I now rest here, in this bliss?
To call him, love him, always kiss?
Was I his one, his only girl?

The one he loved in this huge world?
I looked at him and caught his eye
He smiled at me, I had to sigh...
He was my boyfriend, I was his girl
He was my life, I was his pearl.

A Thousand Lights

There was a night when we did see
A thousand lights combust and bleed
Across the sky like shooting stars
We screamed at once with booms and "wows!!"
You held me close with arms around
My waist and hips, I heard your sounds
You heard me laugh and "oooo" and ah
You laughed with me, I kissed your paw.
I'd never been to this "Kaboom"
So many people couldn't move!
You found a place up on a hill
We climbed up fast and then stood still
To hear the boom the hiss the bang
To feel the thrill of life in hand
How many years I'd longed to see
Some fireworks just you and me
Firecrackers-- in the sky!
We watched them scream and leap and fly!
This glow of lights upon our face
Made love to us and left its trace
Of thrills and chills and joy and laughter
I loved you then and ever after.

Closet Space

You brought your things that filled a jeep
Some hockey gear, some clothes to keep
I made a space within my walls
A closet space quite long and tall
I moved my clothes, some bags, and shoes
I hoped it would be fine with you
Until you'd leave away to Spain
--To work abroad. I felt this pain
Within my chest that wouldn't stop
How could you leave? My heart did drop.
You stayed with me for many days
And I held on, in many ways.
You made me love you and your arms
Your legs, your chest, your scent, your charms
It was at night that I did fall, in love
again each night and crawl
Into your body warm and smooth
In your caress I did approve
It was addictive, this hold of yours
That made me show how one adores
No matter what the day was like
With spats or laughter, daily strife
The night was ours to reconcile
It only took a little while
Your kisses and your hold so tight
Was it because you'd leave one night?
These spoons we laid as on our bed

Kept us as one, from toe to head
I couldn't sleep without you near
But with you, I could dream for years.
And though you left, your heart did burn!
Your love for me, made you return.

Pucking Around

My love could play hockey, just like a young lad
He had his gold trophies, his skates and knee pads.
He played with his friends and other fine skaters
I cheered for my love and kissed him much later
He played on cold ice in green and white gear
And smiled so sweetly, whenever he'd near
He'd kiss me at breaks all sweaty and sweet
I whistled so loudly, like birds I could tweet!
My love would go crashing against his opponent
I learned many words like --- goal, foul and atonement.
He flashed right to left and down to the other
I watched him feel power, without any bother
From other opponents who crashed into him
He wanted to score! He wanted to win!
This glory he felt, this passion and goal
Was all the more reason to love his sweet soul
I watched my love race and shoot and fall over
I watched him get up and feel his sore shoulder
But nothing would stop, this boy-man from steering
His life was his game, as his "fan"
I keep cheering!

The Call

When night is day and day is dark
And hope is lost without a spark
There is one voice that takes away
The body stilts that make one stay
Upright and strong or else they'll see
That you're as weak as none should be
As strong and tall and with it all
Thank goodness for your voice your call
I heard your voice crack on the line
You felt my pain, your pain was mine
You were supposed to go to Spain
From California, now this pain
Had made you stop right in your tracks
You didn't even stop to pack
You took a drive down sunshine state
Then took a plane and kept our date
No sleep, less food, a journey long
I needed you to be so strong!
I came from Rye with Dad that day
And brought him in a peaceful way
Death takes from us that still are here
I couldn't wait for you my dear.
I had to be the strong one then
My mother suffered her loss when
My father died from who knows what…
A bloody brain, a hemorrhage cut
I couldn't grieve, I couldn't cry

I couldn't think... Did he just die?
I didn't have the time to stop
Or think or cry, not one last drop...
Until I heard your voice that day
So far from me, so far away
I told the story to your ear
I couldn't yet believe it dear.
You cried with me and yes, I knew
That he was gone, my pain, it grew.
Now this great man, whom I loved most
Had left me lonely with a ghost
But you came back! To love me here!
I couldn't thank you more my dear!
Your touch, your look, your gentleness,
Was what I needed, in that mess.
You left your plans to be with me
Forever grateful would I be.
I didn't know how to react
And who to hug and help with tact
So many people, so many faces,
Things to do and going places
Family, friends, churches, morgues,
Funeral parlors, hospitals, Lord!
Thank you my sweet for all your love.
You came to me
From up above.

The Painting

We painted beach scenes yellow, blue
Mine was too calm, but yours was true
You moved your paint like no one else
Quick and loose, within yourself
It had a rhythm all its own
Like choppy waters rougher tone
Mine was placid, calm and sad
Yours was brightly colored, mad
Mine was sunset, sullen sweet
Yours was choppy waters deep
You knew, what I was all about
My painting mourned, without a doubt
My father died just days before
You knew about this moving floor
See, you go crazy when someone dies
There is no answer for your cries
For someone's gone but in the wind
They swirl around when waves begin
You stood and listened there once more
Your father died a year before
You knew that I was crazy too
You'd heard the voices and you knew
These crazy waves, they would subside
The voices, terrors, pains inside...
This painting's waves were fierce and wild
The trees did sway when winds weren't mild
But white waves swished beneath our step

And tossed us down through darkest depths
Oh, this was surely frightening
Until waves tossed us up to breath
And then we laughed and then we knew
That we were one, afloat on blue

Faith

There was a young boy who came from the South
He had green eyes, and a round little mouth
He could not speak, our native tongue
But math he loved, since he was young
He played a part, in our school play
And gave a growl a wolf would say.
He learned to read his English well
He used his brain and aced with skill
He went to learn from those who knew
This boy was special, this boy was true
For he believed he'd find success
He studied, he learned, he gave it his best
I never knew, what he would become
Until thirteen years when I heard from someone
The news that this boy who came from afar
Let teachers know, he'd become quite a star
A graduate student from scholarly places
An engineer honored among many faces
This boy gave his thanks for teachers that day
"You believed in me, teachers, showed me the way!
You kept me from doubt, with your solid Faith
Thank you dear teachers, for loving this way!"

2003 miles

This long distance thing, it takes from one's life
The joy and the hugs, the passion and strife
No feeling or touching, no long talks in bed
Just thinking and missing and pining instead.
I wanted you back and spoke to you often
This distance was nails that sealed my coffin
You came back to see me, for weeks at a time
But still there'd be endings as time did go by
I wanted a boyfriend, a love, and a man
To stay by my side, to dream of our plan
To live in a house with children and pets
To sleep in one bed to be ever-blessed
But you'd go away to life in the woods
I missed you so much but you understood
That I would be here to love you once more
And saw you again at my lonely door.

The Bike Ride

"You're out of shape!" You said to me
I wanted you, to let me be
To battle up these Cisco streets
That swerved and curved and made me scream!
We were supposed to cross the park
From the big bridge with crimsoned arch
Where we could sit and kiss and talk
And hug a bit but we were cross
So many miles were crossed that day
This did not seem, to go your way
But we did stand upon the bridge
The sun set down upon a ridge...
The bikers screamed,"Hey! To your left!"
They yelled at me, for I seemed deaf!
I was afraid of their fast pace!
While you just rode with peaceful grace...

We walked our bikes back to our home
You cried for moments once alone
So sad you were that I was sad
You thought that I was really mad
So then I tried to get you out
Of sadness and of dreadful doubt
For even though my legs were beat
I loved you more for thoughts so sweet
To ride with me across the land
Together riding hand in hand

Your plan had spoiled but so what?
In bed we rested still in love.

"Hey, Kiss me," did I tell you then
And kiss we did 'til night did end.

West Coast

The land was picturesque my dear
The trees were tall and steep I feared
I'd never driven through a tree
I stayed within your jeep to see
I took my photographs of leafy green
And saw a painting never seen
Life sparkled in the chartreuse light
Dew glistened on the ferns and pines
The rockslides were a threat to some
But you just drove and sang your song
The rivers ran quite quickly by
I'd never seen such beauty sigh
The road took us to Redwood's town
The giant gods seemed to look down
The next day we went west to see
Pacific Ocean, could it be!?
The cracks around the rocky beach
Brought waterfalls within our reach
The sand was cool, the water calm
You walked with me, and sang your song
A lonely cave was round the bend
I wanted to make love just then
The next day we went to the tubs
With water warm and sky above
You sat upon the edge and asked
Me to be kind and then you basked
I loved you for a while there...

Then you came in the bath and stared
You brought your loving hands to me
And fingers felt me warm and clean
It hadn't been an hour yet
Our naked selves were smooth and wet
The time was up, we had to go
I kissed you soft, you kissed me slow...

The Pool

At Francis Ford's big pool
Where we had gone to swim
We had no reservations
And so you made one then…

For some time in the future,
The next time we would come
I was so glad to think
Of future plans in sun

It wasn't meant to be
This swimming day with you
For now I'm in your past
Our story is now through

We never went to swim
When June did come around
But on your phone one day
It made a little sound

It sent you a reminder
Of what you were to do…
At least you thought of me
And times of love once true

Daily Walk

The nights were ours to speak, with miles in between
I knew your every step, before I went to bed
You started down the street, so black and very steep
I worried for your life, as if I was your wife
So onto college lane, where people were enchained
In studies about trees with cannabis to please
With miles left to go, you traveled to and fro
While cars sped past your frame, I spoke to say your name
You walked up to the bridge and crossed the highway ridge
The cars would never stop, my heart, it often dropped
A little further more you walked past little stores
And looked upon the square, just past the theater there
Then lastly you would go and drink a beverage cold
These spirits and these games would entertain your brain
The Hockey game was on; the juke box played a song,
That made you think of me and all our history
You had to write my name; but texting's not the same…
I never left the phone, for then I'd be alone
You texted me that night to let me know your plight
Of how you wished I had, moved with you…I was sad.
I should have gone with you, to live a year or two
And maybe we could then, be true to love again.
You called me every night to take away my fright
I wouldn't go to sleep until I heard the ping
That came out of my phone, to tell me you were home
I had to hear your voice, my heart gave little choice
I had to hear it near, my loving desperate ear.

I still long for the sound, of you with cars around
And sometimes when I want, I hear a message haunt
From voicemail on my phone, to feel less alone
I'll never lose that sound, in my heart you resound
From nights when we did speak, with miles in between

Love notes

When I was young, I sang so well
I fell quite under music's spell
I sang my heart in choir loft
And sang my prayers sweet and soft
Then when I grew, I sang some more
Took singing lessons, learned my score
I sang Maria, Rosie, too
I won at contests, this is true!
But when I said that Oper-a
Was something that I really loved
You gave a statement sad for me
"Opera's pretentious, can't you see?"
I tried to make you understand
But you loved mostly jazzy bands
I was afraid to say much more
You walked away from me so sore
I took a breath so I could say
My thoughts on how you felt that day.
"If you could feel what I have felt
From music's love that made me melt
You'd know the joy that music brings
It takes you in and makes you sing!
Just as you feel when jazz does move
Your heart and head to make you groove

See, we could meet on middle ground
And understand this glorious sound
Uplifts the soul and understands
That love is made with music's hands."

Morning

Sleepy eyes, soft cool thighs, moistened lips, moving hips
Searching hands, nipples stand,
spooning chest, gasping breath
Breathing in, head then spins, hands in hair, love's kiss fair
Tongues embrace; kiss your face, here
and there... Everywhere
Down you go for your show, feeling high--- breathing slow
Voices rise, feeling size, penetrate, no debate
Moving fast, make it last! Get on top---- Please don't stop!
Sweating now, OH and how! Kiss my neck, feel my wet...
Hold my hands, lover's lands, thighs still clasp in your grasp
Morning cries, gasping sighs, Love,
love, LOVE!!! Scream above!!!!

Silent now
Feeling how
Lover's make
Morning Quake

Again?

Came to find you missed me too, when
you snuggled me like new
I did question how we came, to this comfort once again.
Clasping hands and firm embrace,
waking up to your warm face
Nestled in my neck and form, felt you
breathing soft and warm
Slept we did 'til morning bone, then
your fingers made me moan,
People slept in other places, while we kissed each other's faces
How I wanted you, that day, in that bed and in that way!
But
We were friends, that's what you said,
here upon this crumpled bed
Wishes for your love just then, made
me want you back again.
But I played it cool until, music filled my heart and will
Dancing, singing, singing loud, underneath a mid-day cloud
Singing songs we'd heard before, I did cry at every score
You were happy, I could see, because happy, you made me
'Twas your goal that very day, to give me, a chance to say
That I loved you, but you knew, and
you loved me, you did too!
Why do men play all these games?
Saying, they don't want to stay
But they finger our warm thighs and
between what does surprise

Free wet love is all about, what men like, there is no doubt
So should women let them play with
our souls or should we say
"Love my body, love my soul, both
are one-- if not, then go."

Blowhole

In the woods there is a place, where one
crawls through nature's space
First through trees with sunlit moss,
bursting green with morning frost
Fairies surely watched us walk through
those trees that seemed to talk
Whisper-ing their fairy tale of our love so rare and frail
Pathways came from here and there
'Til we saw tall grasses rare
You pulled back, the tallest ones, to
give space for me to come
Walls of branches grabbed my coat, pushing to a larger moat
Quite a castle did it seem, as we came into this dream
Orange sand did make this fort, leaning towers for our court
Then I stood by sea and sky looking out upon to sigh
Crashing waves did reach to us, bursting flames of watery lust
Loving land with her embrace, casting kisses on her face
Water thrust throughout the chasm, pushing
through with blasting spasms
Flash of white and groaning quake,
surged to heights of mortal ache!

For the love so close to me, on this castle by the sea

Thirsty

Just a man of thirty-two, came to me, like me to you
Asking me to be His friend, at a well where I could send
Down a bucket for my thirst, into darkness, my own curse
"That won't help you" said the man.
"You should have another plan."
"I don't know you," I told Him. "Yes, you do and other men.
More than four have come and gone.
Now you're with another one,"
How He knew this, I knew not. Could
he be the One I sought?
"I don't know you,"
"Yes, you do. I can save your life for you,"
"I'm still thirsty, let me be!"
"You won't thirst if you know Me..."
"Aren't you just another one, who comes
and goes when he is done?"

"I am, I was, and I will be, the One
who comes to set you free.
I don't love, the way men do. I come
to quench your thirst for you.
Yes, you seek, for love out there, but
real love... it does not care,
For human lust, or flighty friends, these
things, they start, and only end.

See, I will quench your thirst today.
But please don't give your love away,
To those who'll never love you right.

Drink of God's love, His pouring light"

Fake Smile

Going out alone,
Is torture with a groan
You pretty up your face
And take a breath with grace
You walk out of your door
And drive to somewhere for…
A moment to be out
And see what life's about
You put on your best smile
And hope that in a while
Some man will come along
And say that you belong
This human race is large
So someone must be ours
To love and to behold,
Before we get too old
But every night that I
Walk out into the light
I'm wishing for the day,
When pain will go away
For nowhere not in sight
Is there a love to light
This darkness everywhere,
That swallows up my air
So back to bed I go
To lay again alone
And hope that sleep will take,

My loneliness away
What hope is there for me?
When loneliness can be
The way I end each night
And lose my little light
I guess I'll have to see,
What happiness can be
When spring will reign once more
And I will be adored

Inferno

A fire burned in front of home
My mother witnessed, all alone
The grass lit up with burning flame
The men made haste to keep it tame
They sprayed the grass with water quick!
It spread like lightning across the strip
Of land that sat before my home
Destroying life and grass and stone
Had someone cursed this patch of grass
That grew each year in spring's sweet grasp?
Had someone cursed this fire to burn
To kill and make Inferno churn?
The aftermath was black and dead
It made the view seem lost with dread
Such mass destruction blackened Earth
Had left a mark of darkened mirth
For days I came home to this sight
To burnt dark grass, to blackened life
But then a shining blade of grass
Burst through the ash that would not last
The ash did feed the soil with food
And caused the grass to grow and shoot
Up from the ground like fruit of Earth
It knew the way to life's rebirth!

So now I look and see the grass
And see the patch where once was black
To my surprise these blades of green
Now grow much brighter than once seemed.

Memories of Summer

Camping in hills, near cold Frio's bend
Made Father and I, the truest of friends
We gathered dry wood and camped in the trees
Eating our lunch of baloney and cheese
The cold river rushed, into the rapids,
That caused quite a splash with no water placid.
I sat in my float, pushing away
From rocks in the bank and started that day
To float on the river and look at the sky
That hovered above and made me feel high
We came to the spot where tree roots did snarl
And saw the white water, as my float did crawl
Slowly advancing, causing some fear
The rapids were sucking my inner tube near!
Swish went my body in anticipation
Feeling the pull of this splashing location
Rocking and bumping, my inner tube went
Taking my body through abandonment!
Water was splashing all over my face
Making me blind, with increasing pace!!

Just about then and right about noon,
I began to float to a dark, deep lagoon
Clear as the sky, the water appeared
Here I would dive, in deep water clear

Daddy was near and still being tossed
By white, rushing water, His laugh came across
The sky that beheld us, with its sunlight giver
In that Frio Water, at Garner's clear river

Memories of Capri

Mom and I sat for a while
And asked if we could drink a vile
Of lemoncello, smooth and sweet
(We hadn't had a thing to eat)
So bottoms up, we drank our fill
Of yellow fire, brisk and chilled
And then we sat a little more
As Daddy bargained by the shore
They brought another glass to us,
Two lemoncellos, we did trust
To calm our nerves for ferry ride
Was coming on, a bumpy tide
Salud! We laughed and giggled more
We were not really keeping score.
Then Daddy came with quickened pace
He didn't want to make us wait
He found us giggling at waiters cute
We saw him, and became quite mute
He'd caught us being naughty ones
And looked at me, then looked at Mom
He called the waiter back, I think, and
tried this lemoncello drink.
He thought it was a new delight and
bought a bottle for the night.
We giggled, giggled on that boat
And rode the waves to Naple's moat.

Voice

There is a boy who shared my home
So I would not grow up alone
He held me close when I was young
And left our home at twenty-one
He went to make a life out there
To sing his life with voice so fair
His instrument his voice would be
The thing that made his history
I heard his voice a thousand times
In O-pe-ras, and church hymn rhymes
His voice was warm and deep as bells,
The deeper ones that boom and swell
I hadn't heard his voice for months
Until that day and only once
We'd chosen hymns our father loved
For he'd be listening from above
The pain and shock was just too much
For brother mine, his voice to trust
That he could open up his voice
And sing the tune of father's choice.
He sat beside my mother there
And gave her all his love and care
He felt that was his purpose now
And prayed to God as he did bow
But sometimes music lifts the soul,
May torment one to break the goal
To keep inside what must come out

I never even had a doubt...
That on this day, this voice would ring
Into that chapel but to sing!
"How Great thou Art" My father's song,
Did surge through air from brother's lung
His voice did raise all eyes to see
They stopped at once to hear him sing!
The organ played, the leader sang
But brother's voice was what began
All ears to hear, all hearts to raise
Their song to God, their thoughts to praise
"How great Thou Art" this bell did ring!
I'm sure it made my Daddy sing...

I thought you were quite done with me
I said I loved you---you agreed
This other one had been so kind
A friend to take me off your mind
She fit the key to happiness
So why were you still in my mess?
Should you have not gone far away,
to other lands that very day?
Why did you stay within my walls, to
fix my ceiling and my halls?
Why did you take me out for drinks, to
speak to me as friends would think?
Why did you call me on my phone,
and ask me if I'd be at home?
Why did you kiss me soft that day,
before you left and went away?
Why did you make sweet love to me
as I declared my love to thee?
Why did you come that day to eat, to taste
my food, weren't you a cheat?
Why do you now stay quite away, for
months now gone, so far away?
Is it that, too much time has passed, to
make amends for crimes long past?
Or do you think about me still, oh, how
I cried, and screamed at will?
Does the image of that day, when you talked and talked away

When I wept with bottle near
And pled for love, your love so dear
Make you sad for what you did? For
what you had and what you hid?
Then wonder about me, long lost friend
And wonder if we'll meet again
Yes, wonder about me, have no doubt
My life goes on
With you
Without

Mother

They say that those who cannot-- teach
I guess I am the one to preach
To parents who have little ones,
Just versions of themselves, begun
I wanted love that was the truth, a
husband in my former youth
But babies were a paradox, a crying thing a voice with locks
I saw my cousins lose their youth
Their freedom, joy, and body too
So why were they so much in love
with little babies from above?
I never knew this until now, that I'm
so old and lonely wow...
I thought that teaching was a way, to
keep from ever wanting babes
But lately I desire things, a family, a home, a ring
A child with curls around its head
With eyes like yours who laughs in bed
I wonder how we'd be as one, a family of love and fun
That day we took your niece to dine,
The waitress thought that she was mine
How could it be that child so rare could
love me as a mother fair?
I looked at you and I could see the
happiness between us three.
So though I teach and yes I do,
I'd love to be a mother too.

Everyday

Feed Cat, soft fur, need nap, sweet purr
Mom calls, day cap, church things, long nap
Eat eggs, eat berries, clean up, want cherries
News tales, show half, world's fucked, must laugh
Treadmill, long stretch, yoga, deep breath
Stand straight, one leg, forget, life's threats
Take bath, or shower, sweet smells, scent power,
Dry off, pet cat, breathe deep, recap.
Find bed, take pen, write down and then
Read book, too late, must sleep; make haste, to dream, again
Good day, same end

J

She suffered long with painful bouts
of being lost and tossed about
Until one day when spring was ended and
summer's sun gave love pretended
For summer joy is like a song which
sings in warmth but not for long
They walked in nature's warming glow
and loved their lives as he foretold
Through all those years that she did feel,
his love was true and free and real
But, sometimes feelings do betray, from
seeing truth become dismay
She writhed in pain, with tears and wails
Her face was gray and sad and pale
He tried his best to tell her all, but
was too late to break the fall
For when one woman strikes the heart
The other woman falls apart
The wound was great the love was too
But sometimes truth is all too cruel
Away he went and she did brew, they spoke no words
But thoughts they grew
She heard his voice
In other lands call out her name in wind and sand
She wanted to, go out to him, but fear
and pain made walls begin.

Perhaps one day when fires are out, when
smoke is gone with ash and doubt
She will return to him that day, to
hold his hand, take pain away
And he will feel her hand forgive, to love,
to hold, and once more live.

Waiting

Winter's thrall to April's spring, bringing
hope to thoughts unseen
Colder winds still kill the joy
Of a springtime, nature's toy
Freezing cold in April's day
Winter clothes still warm the way
People dress to keep their warmth,
waiting for a summer storm,
Hands are cold and toes are too
Wearing robes and slippers blue
Spring is here so why is this
Such a cold and absent kiss?
Wasn't spring supposed to bring, flowers, showers, and a ring?
Am I waiting for a dream
That will never thus be seen?
Am I waiting here in vain for this Spring to come again?
Still I wait for Spring to come
For some warmth to come along
Has this Spring forgotten me?
Left me cold to let me be?
Am I hopeful but insane,
Is Spring drowned in constant rain?
Am I frozen, far too cold…Is it done, this story told?
Waiting for a true hot day,
Winter please just go away.

No more

No more drunken fighting cries
No more tipsy buzzing sighs
No more waking up at two
No more loving, cuddling you
No more smoking in the car
No more driving under stars
No more you to hog the water
No more sharing loving shower
No more running round the town
No more being, driven around
No more crazy airports, cars
No more flights to where you are
No more eating Tex-Mex food
No more sharing food with you
No more jealousy of girls
No more you, within my world
No more freezing at your games
No more cheering out your name
No more rush at Christmas time
No more man to call you mine
No more ties to keep me down
No more arms to wrap around
No more yelling in the car
No more sunset skies afar
No more angry jealousy
No more caring about me
No more calls at 1 am

No more calls to hear my name
No more pain and no more shouts

How I loved you
No more doubts

Mother

Met her forty eight ago
In her belly down below
She was married to my dad
Ready for her girl so glad
Took me home when I was born
I was born one August morn
Looked at mom and loved her more
than I've ever loved before
Now I see my mommy dear
Living closely by and near
We are friends and family
With Earth's loving gravity
Life is hard and sad sometimes
But my mother calms my mind
I will always love her for...
She's the one who loved me more.

Release

For bringing darkness into light
I forgive with flame so bright

For taking what you thought was yours
I forgive from open doors

For flaunting happiness at me,
I forgive with love to be

For bringing tears for thoughtless stealing
I forgive with cleansing healing

For piercing a soul, now pulled apart
I forgive with an open heart

For bringing me to my bleeding knees
I forgive from angel's wings

For not knowing, what you caused
I forgive for pain that was.

Love is...

A mother's constant text or call, a moment just to hear it all

A kitty's purr when mother pets her loving fur when baby lets

A friend who listens far away, the one
you know will let you stay

A gentle smile from children friends whose
lives you watch as they begin

An older friend who judges not, Who
worries some, sometimes a lot

A leader wise who wonders what, there
underlies in your deep thoughts

A Father gone who sits and waits to see
you smile from heaven's gates

A friendly choir who prays and sings in
times so dire—makes my soul ring!

A healing hand that works away, the
stresses from the darkening day

A gentleman who'll dance away the night
with you and make your day

A group of girls who sit and talk to tell
their tales when others walk

A memory dear that throws you back to
Better days before all cracked

A God above who sends you flowers through
friends who love in darkest hours

A confidant who listens, cries, and
makes you laugh at other's lies

A trip to sea to laugh out loud to let all be, to be a cloud

A moments cry to give yourself the
strength to live, to love yourself

Summer

Sleeping late and lying naked
Kitty purrs for breakfast, "Make it!"

Waking up whenever- time
Making up my lazy mind

Reaching for the phone to see
Whose birthday is it going to be?

Rolling over, get up soon
Life is lazy until noon

Breakfast time, relaxing too
I eat outside, enjoy the view

Life is calm and peaceful now
Got through winter's hell somehow

No more searching in the night
Pillows fill that space just right

I swim, I play, I laugh out loud
I think of me and make me proud

The scars will show from time to time
But love will brighten up their grime

I'm warmer now and feeling new
I've got so many things to do!

But until then, breathe in breathe out

I thank the sun for coming out

Printed in the United States
By Bookmasters